The  of Golf Limericks

**By
David Hench**

Copyright © 2018 David S. Hench

All rights reserved. No part of this publication may be reproduced without the prior written consent of the copyright owner.

ISBN: 978-1985318922

Revised Edition

Cover sketch by
Whitney Leigh Carpenter
Louisville, Kentucky

Illustrations by
Whitney Leigh Carpenter
Louisville, Kentucky
and
Brian Dickson
The Villages, FL

The Little Book of Golf Limericks

Funny Golf Limericks

Fabulous one-of-a-kind brief "stories in rhyme" about the great game of golf.

A limerick is kind of a smart-aleck story
But not mean spirited or defamatory
Just a playful jest
To whom it's addressed
And a punchline is most mandatory!

Now ... on to the golf limericks!

A Tricky Putter Indeed!

__Golf Funnies__

A masochist golfer on his blog
Did really cut through the fog
He was far from dumb
And noted with aplomb
That "golf" spelled backwards is "flog."

A coveted birdie is one under par
And an eagle is 2-under out thar
If you play minus three
That's an albatross for thee
But at 4-under we call the golf czar.

They teased him about his spiffy plus fours
Of which he quipped, "The pleasure is all yours"
They continued to make fun
And right there under the sun
He took 'em off and played in his drawers!

The golf course is a good place to meet
For camaraderie it's just hard to beat
Be sure to take care
To be diplomatic out there
If the boss goes down to defeat.

A fairly good golfer named Steven
Made the turn at level par … even
He blew up on the back
Really blew his stack
His clubs in the lake he was heaving!

A hacker took shot after shot
It added up to really quite a lot
At time to enter his score
At the club house he yelled "Fore"
"How do I know?" said he, "I forgot."

He was the longest hitter I assure
But somehow he just couldn't score
It rarely went straight
His unfortunate fate
Was his perennial exclamation of "Fore!"

Golf Limericks

A duffer got stuck in a trap
It turned into quite a mishap
It was quicksand you see
And most fatefully
Nothing was left but his cap!

A "hazard" can be a dangerous place
I guess it says so right on its face
Inside the red line at a pond
He would never abscond
Those gators they don't leave a trace!

"What's the course record?" he did ask
Perhaps in glory to bask
But it wasn't the low
He wanted to know
He shot 306 now that's quite a task.

The loveliest golfer of all
Gazed in the mirror on her bedroom wall
"Who is the best?"
She gave it the test
"Not you," it said ... and she moved it out in the hall.

A golfer was on her cell phone
Driving her cart all alone
My goodness sake
She drove into a lake
And to the starter she now must atone.

Right when stroking a key birdie putt
I tell ya you'll never guess what
A cell phone rang
He gave it a bang
It went clear off the green, that's what!

Can you believe your foe's handicap?
Well, you better not in a snap
Best do some research
Or get caught in the lurch
Cause they might be a bit full of crap!

A golfer disappeared at the turn
And all took a moment to mourn
Where did he go?
We really don't know
The world still awaits his return.

Into the woods he went
Oh, the money he spent
On lost golf balls
The total appalls
In the national debt it would make quite a dent!

A duffer 3-putted six holes in a row
In the process lost some considerable dough
He went to Gambler's anonymous
Which now is eponymous
Oh my! ... say it ain't so.

They say the game can drive you crazy
Or at least make your gray matter hazy
It can get under your skin
Make you swear (that's a sin)
If you keep your wits at all times you're a daisy!

Among golfers it's quite untoward
More vicious than pen or the sword…
Is the sacrilegious claim
If you take dead aim
And say golf is a four-letter word.

The longest course ever seen
Was a truly epic eighteen
Number 1 was in Maine
The turn was in Spain
And the 19th hole was Argentine!

My first three went in the lake
My next was a worser mistake
I swung and I missed
And got so summarily pissed
I cussed the golf gods as I spake!

I'm normally a man of my wordy
But that only goes so far, dear Lordy
I hit two out of bounds
On a hole in one of my rounds
But on the scorecard I wrote down a birdie.

I wish I could hit it real far
I wish I was a TV golf star
Wish I could, wish I might
My game is the ugliest sight
I wish I could at least make a par!

You've never seen so many bogies
By a bunch of codgers and fogeys
It was a senior's event
And afterward they went
To the 19th hole and feasted on hoagies.

"Life must be lived as play"
"You can learn more about a person in an hour of play than in a year of conversation" - *Plato*

*(from the famous Mark Twain quote)
**If golf is a good walk spoiled
And not a refuge from the hours we toiled
Consider the source
If your opinion is the reverse
Was Twain's gray matter hardboiled?**

After this one hole I didn't light up a stogey
Not this esteemed, retired old fogey
Two dozen strokes
Pardon me folks
But that's a historic tri-septuple bogie.
(True story!)

(Another true story)
We played seven in a group one day
That's too many you say?
What you don't know
Is one didn't show
There were eight of us scheduled to play!

David Hench

Golf Limericks

Golfers are known to be half insane
Or at least a bit light in the brain
Don't get in their way
When it's tee time day
To stop them you'll need a slight hurricane!

A duffer changed his putter each week
A magic wand he did vainly seek
He 3-putted with them all
Then took them back to the mall
His cranium was kind of oblique.

A hacker bought new equipment each year
But it wasn't the clubs, I fear
He ran out of dough
And quit playing, you know
Now he plays ping pong, I hear.

David Hench

He thought he was dying of thirst
But that wasn't even the worst
The ambassadors are bears
And all over out theres
There's no beer allowed on this course!

He whacked yet again into the wood
Where he didn't do what he should
He foot-wedged around a tree
Put it up on a tee
And knocked it on the green real good!

Golf Limericks

One ambassador was a bit of a tough
If you took the cart out of the rough
He'd fire one warning shot
Then cuss you a lot
His rulings were certainly no bluff.

I heard this one day I'm confessin'
When a golf pro was giving a lesson
"Cure my slice or I won't pay"
The customer did say
I guess it comes with the bloody profession.

After all of the hacks and the dubs
A hacker decided it was his clubs
He forked out the money
Boy it was funny
He played even worse and his ego it rubs.

David Hench

Please don't accuse me of the cheat
Though I'd rather have a good score than eat
In golf I don't fudge
But I do hold a grudge
Of duels over honor history is replete.

Golf Limericks

The best club in my bag is my math
Whence what I say is the score that I hath
    Don't shake your head
    You hear what I said?
Or you'll incite my uncommon wrath!

I was addressing with my trusty 7-iron
When off went the storm warning siren
    I hit a dead shank
    With the siren to thank
That superintendent I hope they be firing!

I loved my gap wedge til it broke
Now my 60 yard game is a yoke
    Why a one hundred shooter
    I'll google on my computer
Has a gap wedge is some kind of joke.

You really shouldn't have a favorite club
Cause if you do here is the rub
You'll use it all the time
And that's not sublime
So when it keeps calling you give it a snub.

Have you ever been hitting 7 on the tee?
It darn sure happened to me
I hit three in the lake
What score did I take?
An even dozen was the final decree.

He hit two out of bounds and four in the lake
Three swings and misses he did take
All on one hole
He was hard to console
It was a Guinness Book Record outbreak!

Golf Limericks

A peculiar thing is the golf course story
Though there are some miscalculations I worry
As with fish tales
From Florida to Wales
They all suspiciously end up in glory!

David Hench

A hacker made 18 birdies one day
How'd he do that, you say?
His rules weren't too picky
In fact kind of tricky
For he had 86 mulligans in play!

He stood over his putt for so long
It was completely, ridiculously wrong
His better half couldn't wait
His longsuffering mate
She struck the proverbial gong.

I never cheat on the links
But sometimes life calls for hijinks
Then there's the case of my memory
Which is a little bit tremory
But I'm as honest as Abe and the Sphinx!

Not to give the reader a jolt
But this is a story of the golf god's power volt
A cheater they say
Got in its way
He was fried by a just lightning bolt!

They continued to play in the rain
His low score in the works, it was insane
It was torrential and dark
Floating by came an ark
When the world is ending golf is in vain!

How many strokes did you take?
Let's see, two went in the lake …
Another was lost
How many strokes does that cost?
Math gives me a pounding headache!

The poor guy got in a sand trap
Well, he didn't get out in a snap
He hacked six times all about
But never got out
It ruined his whole handicap!

There once was a man named Jack
On the golf course he was really a hack
One day he went low
Made two hole-in-ones in a row
And dropped dead from a bad heart attack!

David Hench

A terrible storm hit the course
The lightning just kept getting worse
Off went the siren
He grabbed his 1-iron*
But god zapped him right there on the course!
*(They say even god can't hit a 1-iron but apparently are wrong!)

Golf Limericks

The senior golfer offered up a prayer
And The Almighty said, "How do you dare?
I hadn't heard from you
Since 1962
You're on your own with that shot, so there!"

Golfing and drinking is not too spry
And here is one reason why
He kept swerving the cart
And his group did their part
They gave him a citizens arrest DUI!

Every shot was a hook or a slice
This game isn't always real nice
For the most of us
It will really make you cuss
Is golf a game or a confounded vice!

A port-a-potty right off the green
Was the regrettable unlikely scene
Of my first kidney stone
Boy did I moan
It darn sure was most unforeseen.

A tee time is an escape from the grind
Where the masses can leave their troubles behind
It's off to the links
When the putts they sinks
Is the best consolation they can find.

A group shot blind to the green
Where a foursome was putting unseen
All their balls they stole
As they departed the hole
It was quite a disastrous 18.

"I'm always unlucky on the 13th hole"
Said the duffer you couldn't console
No matter the course
It only got worse
It's triskaidekaphobia he's got in his soul!

What some golfers really shot you don't know
Regardless of what their scorecards show
It says this or that
I'm no diplomat
They're a little like old Pinocchio!

(for crossover poker enthusiasts)
Poker is a game of the odds
And cards and people and ipods
And dealers and chips
Caustic comments and quips
And a dash of the mercurial card gods.

You could fill up one of those Brinks
With the equipment they buy for the links
But you can't buy a good score
From a golf super store
Instead practice some more methinks.

I almost got closest to the pin
It was a brand new bag I would win
The last player of the shotgun
Made a darned hole-in-one
A most blasphemous iniquitous sin!

On the front nine a hacker shot 37
And thought he was nearly in heaven
On the back it got bad
And then downright sad
His final score was 111.

A duffer went off to take a quick leak
And accidentally fell in the creek
There is little doubt
He never came out
His remains they still solemnly seek.

Golf Limericks

A lovely lass was out on the range
When something happened quite strange
   A ball rolled to her feet
   A gent stepped up in heat
Some things they just never change!

The rough was brutal that day
I don't know what else to say
   When a ball got lost
   That was hardly the cost
The whole group got lost in the hay!

David Hench

Golf: The International Game!

Players & Personalities

Arnie was a general of sorts
According to many reports
His army was legion
In most any region
He was a king and a legend of sports.

Johnny Miller often says they choked
Some tempers that definitely provoked
He doesn't sugar coat and lob
That's not his job
But maybe some mercy he could have evoked.

Patty Berg was a phenom they swore
In majors no woman has more
She promoted the game
Make room for this dame
She established the LPGA Tour!

Golf is a game of talent and skill
And resilience, perseverance and will
And decorum and strokes
Of honorable folks
A greater game has not been invented still.

David Hench

Lee Trevino talked a good game
And his playing wasn't too lame
The great "Merry Mex"
From in Dallas, Tex
Swung that stick to his never-ending fame.

The Hawk cut a path through the game
With a steely will that was anything but tame
He was Texan thru and thru
His legend only grew
There was drama when Hogan took aim.

Who was the greatest putter in the game?
Who earned the greatest acclaim?
Watson or Woods?
Was Crenshaw the goods?
Or Chevy Chase of *Caddyshack* fame?

A sportsman all the way to his bones
At the rarest of levels and tones
An original master
This sportsmanship pastor
He's legend. The name: Bobby Jones.

Golf Limericks

The One and only Gary McCord
Is known for an irreverent word
He offers color and quips
And various postscripts
His tongue is sharper than the sword!

The velvety tones of Jim Nantz
On the tube never fail to enhance ...
The viewers' delight
In fact they might
Put the unsuspecting viewer in a trance!

One of the greatest ever who teed
It's enthusiastically, unanimously agreed
Virginia's very own
His record it shone
The Slammin' One ... Samuel J. Snead.

A Buckeye charged on to the scene
To become the greatest there's been
18 in all
It's where he stood tall
In the majors Nicklaus is dean.

This long and lean feminine Swede
Cut a mean vision when she teed
Alfie or Helen
They be a-tellin'
Mrs. Alfredsson has gusto indeed!

On the LPGA scene quite a fixture
A champion, coach and linkster
From Cali Santa Cruz
She hated to lose
That handsome and talented Inkster!

Golf Limericks

At the Masters his famed double eagle
Rendered the man historically regal
It came down to the wire
But went to The Squire
Look it up … it's final and legal.

He outdueled Jack at Turnberry and Pebble Beach
With the great trophies well within reach
Watson's the name
And putting's the game
What he had no golf coach could teach.

The links had a great white shark
His bite was worse than his bark
He had some rough luck
But through all the muck
The Aussie Norman made a huge mark.

A dashing Spaniard appeared in the game
And Pedreña was never the same
So young he left us did Seve
But first he won a bevy
His story is legend in Spain.

South Africa produced this champ
Of the fitness and sand save camp
He won the career grand slam
He passed the exam
On the game Player sure put his stamp.

A sharpshooting feminine Swede
One of the greatest ever it was decreed
A Wildcat in college
For her golfing and knowledge
Annika's an all-time great it's agreed.

Her sporting feats weren't nefarious
Though they most certainly were various
She won gold in track and field
Then the clubs she did wield
I give you Babe Didrikson Zaharias!

This Swedish born queen of number one
Became "Miss 59" before she was done
She won non-stop
And retired on top
The one and only Annika Sorenstam.

An LPGA star worth her salt
She peppered the fairway a lot
When she won the Dinah Shore
You had to adore
Dottie's victorious amphibious assault!

David Hench

One of the guys that was neat
A straighter hitter you never will meet
The man from Detroit
His driver was adroit
The '84 Vardon Trophy winner, Calvin Peete.

Another dashing player from Spain
The 2017 Green Jacket he did attain
A Ryder Cup champ
From the European camp
Can Sergio pull off a refrain?

The wisecracking Irishman of the game
His witty tongue hath garnered him fame
Feherty does kid
But some parts stay hid
He and his alter ego are not the same!

As to the greatest golfer of them all
An argument will always befall
Jones, Nicklaus, Woods?
Who was the goods?
That troika would sure make an historic cabal.

The Old Course at St. Andrews is renowned
As consecrated golfing ground
When it hosts The Open
The contestants are hoping
And ALL of the legends are around!

A Georgia Bulldog lefty clubber
Sure knew how to get out of trouble
With two Masters wins
Knocking down pins
The fast driving phenom named Bubba.

For all of his work on the range
I'm sure he wouldn't exchange
His two U.S. Opens in a row
Those days he went low
Wake Forest's very own Curtis Strange.

"The Big Easy" from Africa came
With coolness and plenty of game
Two Opens each
His record did reach
Golf is the game and Els is his name.

One of the greats was Sir Nick
At Augusta he thrice turned the trick
The British Open too
He won a slew
The majors were his bailiwick.

He hit it 800 miles ... that's long
Commentators said it was just plain wrong
At the '91 PGA
He carried the day
Paul Bunyon (I mean John Daly) was strong.

There once was a lady named Nancy
Her golf game was certainly fancy
She took them by storm
Her smile big and warm
That Lopez was no long shot chancey.

At beautiful famed Pebble Beach
A championship is always in reach
An ethereal sight
And an artist's delight
For how much can a golfer beseech?

David Hench

On the golf course he might be a dope
His handicap wasn't up to the slope
He sure cracked the jokes
And delighted the folks
The incomparable, incredible Bob Hope!

It's hard to beat this stylish Lefty
Golf got his bankroll fairly hefty
With three Masters in tow
And chipping for show
Phil worked those short shots quite deftly.

There once was a sharpshooter name Rory
When he attacked the field it got gory
He'd run off and leave
And grant no reprieve
It's quite an Irish folk story.

The hacking and joking Bill Murray
Scored his triple bogeys in a flurry
With him anything goes
He'll assuage your woes
On the etiquette he's a little bit blurry!

Golf Limericks

At Augusta a hallowed spring rite
A course like no other in sight
At the Masters they gather
There's nowhere they'd rather
A deserving champion is crowned Sunday night.

Golf was a Scottish tradition at first
Then upon Europe it burst
And with the help of TV
That the whole world could see
For the game there's an international thirst.

Golf is a passion in Wales
From where the '91 Master Champ hails
Hip hip for Woosie
He was no floozy
To the jolly good fella happy trails!

David Hench

There once was a lefty … Bob Charles
He was easygoing and not full of snarls
He tore it up in the seniors
The champ from New Zealand
He sure didn't rest on his laurels.

To measure his effect on the game use a Geiger
He glowed red hot as a scrambler and striker
He stalked The Bear
But hasn't got there
But he's second in majors this Tiger.

Hailing From Fiji island here's the thing
This man just crushed with his swing
9 wins in a year
Even a tiger would fear
The golfing phenom Vijay Singh.

That '60s stalwart Billy Casper
Was quite a remarkable lasher
They called him Buffalo Bill
He sure wasn't run of the mill
And in 1970 he was The Master.

Golf Limericks

Hale Irwin was a Buffalo fellow
He was a grinder, not super mellow
Three U.S. Opens he won
Before he was done
The pressure couldn't turn him to gello!

Lord Byron won 11 in a row
A record he'll never let go
Another Texan superstar
In matters of par
There were few who reached his plateau.

Tournament golf is a game of the mind
The pros all say they did find
It's a pure mental test
To see who is best
So to them it's not a game it's a grind.

Sir Walter was a dandy they say
But even that was overshadowed by his play
Eleven majors in the bag
For the indomitable Haig
You know his nickname could have been "Broadway."

Charlie Sifford played his way to fame
And became the Jackie Robinson of this game
He broke the barrier
And is forever the carrier
Of golf's integration and social justice flame.

In the revered annals of the game
Few resonate like two of the same name
Scottish father and son
8 British opens they won
Old and Young Tom Morris sure made their claim.

A Rhodesian streaked into view
This world "Number 1" got his due
Two majors in '94
Are part of his lore
Tis Nick Price's lofty review.

Out of Dallas and Longhorn U.
Is this a king of the hill anew?
There's much to a name
Jordan's are known to have game
What will be writ in the books next to you?

More Funny Business

The course was so slow to play
That the late groups decided to stay
They camped out all night
And when it was light
Finished their round the next day!

It was so hot the round wasn't much fun
A scorcher in the merciless sun
I dare say
Heat stroke was in play
But they all made it okay and were well done.

It was dark when they finished the round
Any shot could barely be found
One gal played better
To her it was no fetter
For her dark play she became most renowned!

Some have a golf addiction
And play virtually without restriction
They play when they're tumoral
Or on the day of their funeral
That's my esteemed prediction.

A guy was heading to the course one day
He just couldn't wait to play
He was going way too fast
A patrolman he flew past
Doing 110 …. now he's in jail I dare say.

Golf Limericks

A gal loved her pretty golf hat
It was fancy enough for the Derby at that
She got a little cross
When she thought it was lost
But her partner had hid it ... the rat!

A gal had her best round one day
And boy was that fun to play
With a coy little smile
She blushed for a while
And said, "That was better than foreplay."

David Hench

Some say a therapy for golf
Is the massage treatment of Rolf
They rub you with cream
Maybe tell you to scream
And get out the frustrations of golf.

On ladies day the caddies rejoiced
Happy sentiments they roundly voiced
Sugar and spice
And everything nice
Is better than what the male ego foists.

He had never broken 80, not once
It was one of his most fervent wants
Finally he did
Of his monkey he was rid
But he didn't want to do it just once!

Many a player said regarding prayer
In golf it won't help you out there
For the guy and the dame
It's such a heavenly game
So how come god doesn't care?

Golf Limericks

There are plenty of examples in golf lore
Of shouting the infamous "fore"
Hitting it five times or more
One or two to ignore
And writing down four on the score.

Golf is a game of good and bad lies…
Of the ball and the gals and the guys
It's the nature of the beast
In diplomacy at least
The hard truth needs a soft compromise.

A couple took a golf honeymoon out west
When asked what about it was best
"I have to say
It was the foreplay"
Both of the duffers confessed.

Watching the golf on TV
I do quite delightfully
Let's watch them sweat
While we just set
And drink our refreshing ice tea.

David Hench

Doctors are known to play
On weekends and on their off day
Best not to get sick
When they are swinging the stick
Or it might be your own doomsday!

He had never broke 70 before
In the game of pins, greens and fore
He finally went low
His face was aglow
In the sixties was his blessed new low score.

A wild hitter named Boarse
Hooked one so far off the course
It caused an affliction
In another jurisdiction
By killing a poor plowing horse!

A lady had to switch skirts at the turn
It wasn't a fashion concern
She had a hole in one
It was showing her bun
And that one she had to adjourn.

A hustler from around about Troon
His gambling was really a boon
He prop bet one day
"I can beat you any old way"
"I'll beat you with an old soup spoon!"
(And he did!)

David Hench

A slicer hit one in the parking lot
White stakes out there there was not
He came out firing
Hit a screaming 3-iron
And put a dent in a red Mazerat!

An old-timer thought he'd made the Guinness Book
So few shots in his round he had took
He did proudly state
He'd shot 28
But it was miniature golf which he partook!

Golf Limericks

Executive par 3s are the rage
They're a more modest links stage
In fact it is so
You can really go low
Par golf is 54, and that's a golfing sage!

There was a wreck on the course, two golf carts
One of the worst ever seen in these parts
There were no broken bones
But four cracked cell phones
"I'm on the phone therefore I am," said Descartes!

He pulled the wrong club from the bag
And let it fly right at the flag
It flew the whole green
Into a ravine
And boy did his countenance sag.

David Hench

A hacker was world-class at "taking" a putt
Of jokes he was often a butt
He played a whole round
It was renowned
His ball never went in the hole, that's what!

A mademoiselle was on a three tier green
The likes of which she had not seen
She tried a long lag
But her plan hit a snag
In reading greens she was hardly the Queen!

A guy stepped up and took a shot
But his turn you see it was not
He got a hole-in-one
But it was no fun
When they ruled it a counterfeit shot.

A lady was putting on the range
When things began to get strange
An alien walked up
Right by the cup
And said, "An interstellar date I can arrange."

Golf Limericks

If you alternate a slice and a hook
I read in a good golf book
That's really bad news
The writer construes
You taking up this game was mistook!

There was a dogleg that turned dead right
This hole was really a sight
It turned 90 degrees
The green, fairway and the tees
It was a flippin' isosceles blight!

I lost my favorite golf hat
In a windstorm that was a real bearcat
It wouldn't stay on
When the storm passed it was gone
I walked the whole course but did not find the hat!

David Hench

I fired a smooth 121
Right out there under the sun
I summarily guessed
You're not too impressed
But surely I can beat someone.

There was an unusual hole shaped like a volcano
It could make you want to drink Drano
A treacherous approach
Ask any golf coach
Then again what do they know?

There was a swinging bridge over a ravine
Like nothing I had ever seen
It swung and it shook
Every step that you took
It was the famed Devil's Bridge, on 18!

I used to have a 3-part backswing
If you've ever seen Barkley, that's the thing
It was such a disaster
For he's a decided non-master
Don't let us take you under our wing!

A foursome disappeared into thin air
It was a mystery what happened out there
It was a metaphysical event
Wherever they went
Some kind of quantum fluctuation most rare!

The long-hitting Alex Pompaduke
One day really pulled off a fluke
A par 5 hole-in-one
A "double albatross" he done
That drive was really a nuke!

David Hench

A Lady at the range looked like a schoolmarm
There was really no cause for alarm
We got introduced
And then I deduced
It was Rebecca of Sunnybrook Farm!

Five brothers went to the links
Most of their games just stinks
They hacked it around
Birdies were unfound
But rivalry was methinks!

Address the ball with a confident stance
And forget there is even a chance
To hit it out of bounds
Ignore all the sounds
Hit long and straight and do your tee dance!
(Submitted by Vic Meenach)

A man played a Nassau who was dead broke
And to some that isn't a joke
I guess he was plucky
Or maybe real lucky
He could have been departed before he awoke!

Back home they would play in the snow
Where the ball was you hardly could know
It was 30 degrees
Your whatchacallit would freeze
Still off to the course they'd go!

David Hench

Hickory, dickory dock
If you hit it to the right it's a block
To the left it's a pull
Golfing can be painful
You might be better off putting your clubs in hock!

A "Bogey" is one over par
Or a Hollywood type superstar
Even though the name
Is spelled just the same
One is less cool by far!

(True story)
I stood over a birdie putt one day
Though it's an unlikely event, you'd say
A tremor hit the ground
An earthquake all around
And my birdie putt shimmied astray!

Golf Limericks

THE CHILDREN WILL JUST HAVE TO WAIT!

One golfer played 700 rounds per year
It was a full-fledged addiction, I fear
It took over his life
Cost him his wife
He didn't know when to say when it would appear.

It's said two or three good shots per round
Will keep the faithful coming around
Back to the course
Til they're in a hearse
Their devotion to the game will abound.

Over a 3-footer a duffer said a prayer
You could hear his knees knocking out there
Golf tests your nerves
You guile and your verves
It can be a nerve wracking disaster, I swear!

Golf must have 10,000 rules
But that's not the design of fools
It keeps shysters straight
Minimizes debate
Except on the 19th hole bar stools!

Golf Limericks

Whilst thumping a golf ball around
My mates made an off-putting sound
I later exclaimed
That the place where I aimed
Was NOT where my golf-ball was found!
(by Brian Dickson)

A golfer had to relieve himself in the trees
But that's where Mr. Bear pees
A fatal mistake
He nearly did make
Luckily the bear was traveling overseas!

A group accidentally played the wrong hole
On their score it took quite a toll
A bunch of penalty shots
Is just what they gots
And the starter put them on parole!

Hickory, dickory dock
On his deathbed a golfer took stock
Any rule he had transgressed
He openly confessed
The golf god thou better not mock!

He used a foot wedge thinking he was alone
The rules he followed were his own
Though he roundly denied
He had been espied
His better half recorded it on her cell phone!

A noise when your partner is hitting is unhealthy
Unless it is teeny, tiny elfie
And it's certainly rude
I hereby conclude
During their shot to be clicking a selfie.

Ladies Day was a popular event
They say a lot less rules got bent
Without all the ego
Of Mister Amigo
And in the golf shop more money was spent.

The club champ got a round of applause
But exactly what was the cause?
It was a 4-putt mock cheer
Among rounds of beer
It was less respect than brutal guffaws!

I kid you not I took 24 putts
On a miniature golf trick hole, that's what's
No ifs, buts or ands
Over all the lands
I guess that makes me the boss mini klutz!

David Hench

At the 19th hole it wasn't right
A loser started a big fight
In golf that's not nice
But he paid the price
He was barred from the course as a blight.

The starter closed down the course
In a storm that could hardly be worse
One player waged on
He didn't want a rain coupon
To stopping play under par he was averse!

Golf Limericks

The greens were so fast you could skate
And that was one poor golfer's fate
As to his score
For skating the dance floor
Since he fell on his ball there was lively debate!

He played an island green down on Hobe Sound
But no trace of him ever was found
He hit so many balls
Sometimes fate befalls
All the balls and the player ... they drowned!

The wind players come out of Texas
And Europe ... that is the nexus
They play it low and straight
It seems almost innate
That goes for both of the sexes.

Sometimes out on the links
Scores are reported with winks
For nature's brush paints
Not many saints
At least in most local precincts!

As rare as the mystical Sphinx
Or the elusive albino lynx
Or a captured Yeti
Or confirmation from SETI
Are those beyond reproach on the links!

The combination of playing the links
And too many spirited drinks
Can get out of hand
You do understand
And lead to regrettable hijinks.

Let a friendly kibitzer keep your card
They might be a creative bard
Maybe your better half
Just for a laugh
Will doctor those numbers real hard!

A golfer found a hidden treasure on number 8
But that was only part of his fate
He was playing in Reno
Stopped by the casino
He went all-in and was a short-lived magnate.

A UFO alighted on number 7
It wasn't a visit from heaven
The course rules instructed
If alien abducted
You were disqualified by number 11.

On number 16 there was a quarrelsome frog
He'd splash the players until they were sogged
Not very nice
An antisocial device
And then he wrote about it on his amphibious blog!

On number 10 was the resident gator
Of golfers he was a hater
He was promptly reported
Then hastily deported
Hey gator we'll see your butt later!

Number 12 had a flock of seagulls
Who picked balls off the greens with their skulls
There were so many penalty shots
That the poor players gots
Now the gulls banishment the green keeper mulls.

Number 14 had a wild badger
That the super just couldn't capture
It caused so much trouble
That right on the double
They hired a professional wildlife dispatcher.

Number 6 on the links had a skunk
To high heaven the cute fellow stunk
When he sprayed the players
All became their naysayers
They were persona non grata that's no bunk!

Golf Limericks

A lovely dame from the states
Was playing in Australia with some new mates
They make a blunder
Around there down under
When her game they underestimates.

Around one course there was a herd of monkey
That were incorrigibly wild and spunky
It sure brought grins
Them swinging on the pins
You think that wasn't so funky?

A course up north had a resident groundhog
A marmot he was called in his book epilogue
A cute kind of critter
Said one big hitter
As to the weather his shadow was prologue!

David Hench

On the range there was a mercurial opossum
Where his darker side really did blossom
He could be meaner than spite
And ready to fight
You best be advised not to cross him!

Down under there was a course Kangaroo
He had some run ins, really quite a few
To golfers he was averse
It could have been worse
If he kicked you we'd bid you adieu!

A dragon got loose on the course
The damage was hard to reverse
A Komodo it was
It caused quite a buzz
They had to call the Malaysian police force!

A bear came out of the wood
And next to the hole it stood
When the next group hit up
And was lagging to the cup
The bear tended the pin ... understood?

Golf Limericks

It was a brutal treacherous island green
Beats all the gallery had seen
He was hitting 21 on the tee
It was frightful to see
Next he dove in and swam his ball to the green.

It was a shotgun scramble event
Some rules they say were really bent
They went absurdly low
But those in the know
Doubted exactly what 72-under meant!

*The wildest hitter in the world, goodness sakes
Yet no penalty shots he ever takes??
What's up with that?
It's really quite a stat
He just couldn't seem to see white stakes.*

The mademoiselle bid her hubby adieu
Because his links trips were quite more than a few
That's one golf lonely heart
That sure did her part
She gave him a bachelorhood sneak preview.

Golf isn't exercise, they parry
It sounds a bit overly contrary
It sure beats the slouch
Who won't leave the couch
Golf's not aerobic but it's not sedentary.

This dude from down south played a hook
With every swing that he took
Right to left, you all
Is where he stood tall
And for a Yankee he was never mistook!

Golf Limericks

His driver head had gotten so big
It would barely stay in the bag, you dig?
When driving about
The infernal thing would flip out
But I guess that's all part of being a bigwig!

A hacker who would sell his soul to break par
And to be a big golfing star
He met with the devil
That's on the level
And they snacked on some French caviar!

A player got anxiety on the tee
He couldn't take the club back, you see?
Since he had froze
The marshall arose
And carried him off in a muscle bound T.

A player was superstitious about washing his ball
It got coated with mud and all
See when it rolled
It hopped and he cajoled
His putting was like a bumpy ground ball.

When it gets down to who would win
Fear, you could say, is a sin
Winners are bold
And when their story is told
Demons of defeat lurk within!

One of my favorite Kentucky courses
Said running around their fairway they had racehorses
Was this the joke
Of which they spoke
When they said there was courses for horses?

We walked into the LCC locker room, five hackers
Brothers all and as big as linebackers
A lifelong member
That chilly November
Said he thought we were the Green Bay Packers!

Twas the hardest course of them all
Listen to this you all
200 was par
Har-dee-har-har
And your handicap it was sure to appall!

Golf Limericks

In the illustrious history of shots
The grand old game of golf has lots
The largest share
Of the peoples out there
Is in the longsuffering land of Scots!

Where Golf Began

Twas the most difficult course of them all
The grounds most surely did sprawl
200 was par
The penalties left a scar
It came with its own wailing wall!

There was an old-timer golfer named Big Jim
You hear all kinds of things about him
Like if you played for money
And don't pay it's not funny
In concrete shoes I hope you can swim!

I dreamed I got smuggled into a PGA event
Maybe some qualifying rules got bent
I started off with the hots
Missed the cut by 200 shots
Then got drunk in the hospitality tent!

Golf Limericks

The Thanksgiving round was windy and wet
And freezing too don't forget
The famed doctor dad
Had never been had
By one of his sons ... but voila an upset!

(*The first time any of us boys had beaten our dad in a golf round. I beat my father by 8 shots, 81-89, on Thanksgiving of 1989 at Lexington Country Club.)

Set your hands low, keep your left arm straight
Keep your head still and transfer your weight
Tuck your elbow too
Inside out and follow through
Oh, never mind all that it's just fate!
(Submitted by Rob Hench)

He had 372 swing thought keys
His anxiety they tried to appease
And they don't even work
Try not to smirk
Is golf a game or a dreaded disease?

David Hench

A dude was 9-under par on the front
For the course record he was on the hunt
He never finished the round
Could never be found
He raptured with the golf gods, that's quite a stunt!

I skulled a sand shot like a dart
Toward my brother who sat in his cart
It went right at his head
That's what I said
I nearly had an attack of the heart!
(*It hit his clubs and fell into his bag of all things!)

A mademoiselle was in a tough spot
Sugar and spice was Miss Dot
But she wasn't as sweet
Her temper took heat
When a quadruple bogey she got!

Night golf was a passion of some
Under the stars they play with aplomb
A par 3 with lights
Is one of golf's delights
A nocturnal golf addict they become.

Golf Limericks

A little rain won't stop me playing

David Hench

A hacker lost 14 balls in one round
None of them his poor caddie found
It could be a record
His past was checkered
And he stole a box of a dozen after the round.

His approach bounded off the pin
It should have almost been in
But it bounced in the lake
A penalty he did take
It almost seemed like a sin.

Golf is an epic sports test
To see whose game is the best
I think you will find
Winning is of the mind
The champions have unanimously confessed.

In golf there is a universal prayer
To the golf gods from players out there
"If you look over my game"
"I'll give you acclaim"
To this I solemnly swear!

Golf Limericks

A mashie, a brassie and a spoon
Filled the old-timer's afternoon
They toiled on the range
You might think it strange
To succeed once in a proverbial blue moon.

FINALLY HIT MY AGE —102!

SOMETIMES THINGS GET NASTY!

Golf grew to include common folk and dames
The most international of games
But once upon a time
Though it now seems a crime
It was outlawed by the regal King James!

The son was a faithful, industrious caddie
But a headstrong opinionated laddie
When he put up a fight
Over which club was right
His player said, "Boy, who's your daddy!?"

Golf Limericks

The ancient European word "kolf"
Sometimes also spelled out as "colf"
You could hear in the pub
That both words meant "club"
And today the spelling is "golf."

A single decided to play through the next group
About etiquette he cared not a hoot
He hit into their green
And the best they could glean
He was some kind of rude nincompoop!

A gent took up the game in France
Where he met a mademoiselle perchance
They fell in love, I'm saying
And out of love with playing
And last were seen at the country club dance.

David Hench

The world's worst player they say
Teed it up from the tips one day
He had taken some lessons
Got the pope's blessings
But he still never hit a fairway!

Lost in the mother of bunkers was he
It was quite a links tragedy
He was playing in Death Valley
Don't ask the final tally
He was lost in the great sands of the Mojave!

A driver was driving her cart on her cell
And that didn't turn out too well
She drove into a bunker
Said, "So what it's a junker"
For driving she won't get a Nobel!

What's the record to get out of the trap?
He hit it 14 times … and then ASAP
He did declare
"This game isn't fair"
And he put the ball in his cap!

David Hench

If you go to hit a shot from a creek
It's not really my place to critique
You might get mud on your face
Or become a disgrace
Or injure your rusty physique.

His scorecard said he shot 40
Which was pretty incredibly sporty
"If you went that low"
St. Pete wanted to know
"Let's see you tell that to the Lordy."

A duffer turned in a smooth 68
"How'd you do that," asked his faithful mate
"I took all the putts ...
These greens drive me nuts ...
So sorry to self-incriminate."

Golf Limericks

Par is 72 you say?
That's not the game I play
Anything in double digits
About 100 with foot widgets
Is more like the game of golf my way!

Those damnable red and white stakes
And lost balls and bunkers and lakes
Seems I find every one
Under the sun
What kind of fun does that makes?

A friend played in Sierra Madre Cali
A beautific mountain and valley
It all was so scenic
Would say all, even Penick
You hardly would care what you tally.

David Hench

They say golf is a game of misses
The game ... all its lovers it disses
But after the round
When we've unwound
It's the good shots which we reminisces.

**On the course some impulses you throttle
Lo, this game can send you to the bottle
I think you will find
It's a game of the mind
And would test the guile of Aristotle!**

Land which gold has besmitten
Where much of the games lore is written
Here, here ... in the isles
For thousands of miles
Hallowed links of Ireland and Britain.

Golf Limericks

HE'S A MEMBER OF THE BOLSHOI GOLF TEAM.

David Hench

The greatest ricochet shot of them all
Careened off Humpty Dumpty's wall
Hit a tree in Liberia
A cart path in Siberia
And bounced stiff to the pin in Nepal!

It was a disastrous world-class misread
A nightmarish horrific misdeed
It rolled off the green
Into an adjacent ravine
Then out of bounds … then it tried to secede!

It was the world's worst lipout putt
3 times around the blammedy cup
The fans were amazed
The putter was dazed
And the ball was laughing out loud straight up!

Back and forth across the green it went
From bunker to bunker it got sent
It stirred up so much sand
You couldn't see land
And the green seemed suddenly absent.

A duffer's putter was 10 feet long
He still couldn't putt worth a song
He was in the 1 percentile
Could plumbbob for a mile
And in golf circles that's just plain wrong.

A particularly sagacious mongoose
On the course was running around on the loose
He occasionally held court
Would offer a tort
And Aristotle he would customarily adduce.

On the green in sunny Florida was a python
Upon which it did slither and writhe on
There were heard screams
And it caused bad dreams
And now the story is a popular icon!

A mademoiselle's ball was so plugged
She was more than a little bit bugged
It went underground
Couldn't be found
And boy she needed to be hugged.

A 100-shooter was calling his shots
Did he have any sense? I have to say nots
He could hardly make a par
But he thought he was a star
His ego precedes him a lots.

Golf Limericks

He took anything inside the leather
But you could have knocked me over with a feather
His putter was so long
It was totally wrong
He took a 10-footer and said "How's the weather?"

I innocently set up a match
Perhaps with too much dispatch
He said he was a hacker
But had a big money backer
And his real handicap was scratch!

A cart was parked on a green by a stranger
Inciting the eternal wrath of the ranger
He barred him away
Forever and a day
The only one who forgives that was born in a manger!

OMG not yet another
A dreaded, exasperating "other"
They catch me off guard
And ruin my card
I can't take much more of them, oh brother!

All These Years and I didn't Know You Could Get Different Lengths of Clubs.

Golf Limericks

He had a huge banana ball slice
In golf that's kind of a vice
All I can say
Is aim left and pray
That's my only word of advice.

It wasn't exactly a treat
When his chip rolled back to his feet
He tried to stay cool
And not act a fool
But his remarks were less than discreet!

On one hole it's bad chili dips
On the next a case of the yips
It's a tortuous game
Impossible to tame
And many days your ego it whips!

David Hench

Humility we all must learn
But her temper started to burn
On green number 10
She lost all her zen
When she putted thrice and did not lose her turn!

On the tee I wasn't the low man
I felt much more like a "po" man
Honors aren't yours
From Scotland to the Azores
When your previous hole is a snowman!

He skulled his intended flop shot
A good shot it certainly was not
It went screaming by
A terrible bullseye
And kneecapped his partner that shot!

They serenade you all over the course
Their singing is in happy full force
A chorus out loud
Audubon would be proud
To the birdies' tunes no ear is averse.

About the Author

Author David Hench is a "limerick laureate" who currently resides in the golf mecca of The Villages, Florida. He is a golf fan, historian, statistician ... even philosopher. He brings together all this into hilariously imaginative little "stories in rhyme" about the game. Some informative, some ridiculous – all entertaining for the golf lover in you!

David Hench

LimerickLaureate@gmail.com

Other books by David Hench:

Hilarious Limericks about being a Senior
Gold in the Soul
Easy on the Soul: Folktales for Adults
The Poker World According to Cinch

Write Your Own Golf Limericks

*(You can do it. This is not Robert Frost stuff!)

Made in the USA
Monee, IL
21 November 2023